Snakes

Anacondas

by Joanne Mattern

Consultant:
Robert T. Mason, PhD
Professor of Zoology
J.C. Braly Curator of Vertebrates
Oregon State University, Corvallis

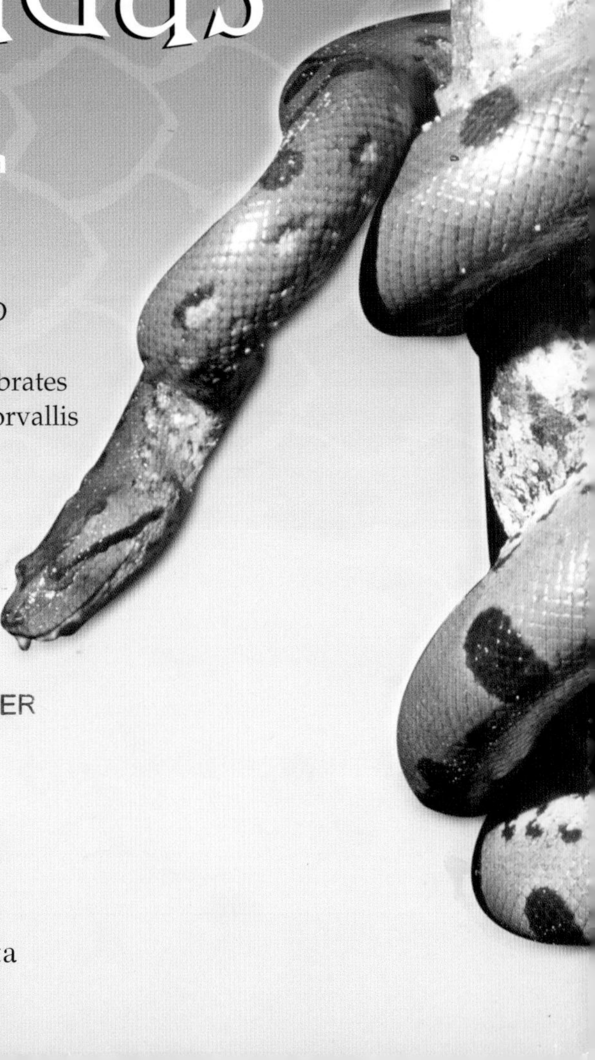

Capstone
press®
Mankato, Minnesota

First Facts is published by Capstone Press,
151 Good Counsel Drive, P.O. Box 669, Mankato, Minnesota 56002.
www.capstonepress.com

Library of Congress Cataloging-in-Publication Data
Mattern, Joanne, 1963–
    Anacondas / by Joanne Mattern.
    p. cm. — (First facts. Snakes)
    Includes bibliographic references and index.
    Summary: "A brief introduction to anacondas, including their habitat, food, and life
cycle" — Provided by publisher.
    ISBN-13: 978-1-4296-1920-2 (hardcover)
    ISBN-10: 1-4296-1920-1 (hardcover)
    1. Anaconda — Juvenile literature. I. Title. II. Series.
QL666.O63M367 2009
597.96'7 — dc22   2007051906

Editorial Credits
Lori Shores, editor; Ted Williams, designer and illustrator; Danielle Ceminsky,
    illustrator; Jo Miller, photo researcher

Photo Credits
Alamy/blickwinkel, 18
Art Life Images/age fotostock/Morales, 8; NHPA/Martin Wendler, 6
BigStockPhoto.com/vladacanon, 11
Bruce Coleman Inc./Erwin & Peggy Bauer, 13; Joe McDonald, 19; M. Freeman, 16
Getty Images Inc./National Geographic/Ed George, 21
McDonald Wildlife Photography/Joe McDonald, 7, 10
Minden Pictures/Ingo Arndt, 5
Nature Picture Library/Jim Clare, cover
Peter Arnold/Biosphoto.Cordier Sylvain, 14–15; Biosphoto/Crocetta Tony, 20; Martha
    Cooper, 1
Shutterstock/Nahimoff, background texture (throughout)

Essential content terms are **bold** and are defined at the bottom of the page where they first appear.

1 2 3 4 5 6 13 12 11 10 09 08

Table of Contents

A Super-Sized Snake

The anaconda is one of the largest snakes on earth. Just how big is it? This snake can grow up to 20 feet (6 meters) long. That's about as long as a garbage truck!

Many big snakes live in the world, but the anaconda is the heaviest. This huge **reptile** can weigh as much as 500 pounds (227 kilograms).

Fun Fact!
Anacondas are easily upset and do not make good pets.

reptile: a cold-blooded animal that breathes air and has a backbone

The Boa Family

Anacondas belong to a family of snakes called boas. Boas kill by constricting. They squeeze an animal until it can no longer breathe.

yellow anaconda

Members of the boa family can be different sizes. Yellow anacondas are only about 6 feet (1.8 meters) long. Green anacondas can grow up to 20 feet (6 meters) long.

Hide and Seek

All snakes are covered with pieces of hard, dry skin called scales. Anacondas' scales make patterns of dark oval patches. Most anacondas have bodies that are green and brown. These patterns and colors help anacondas hide in dark, muddy water. Hiding helps anacondas sneak up on **prey** and stay safe from **predators**.

Fun Fact!
What animal could possibly eat an anaconda? Fierce predators like jaguars do.

prey: an animal hunted by another animal for food
predator: an animal that hunts other animals for food

Anaconda Bodies

Anacondas often lie in sunny places. That's because snakes are **cold-blooded**. Snakes' bodies are only as warm as the air and ground around them.

cold-blooded: having a body temperature that changes with surroundings

nose

An anaconda's nose is on the top of its head. This feature allows anacondas to breathe and smell even when they are swimming.

Anaconda Range

☐ where anacondas live

North America

Europe

Asia

Africa

South America

Australia

Antarctica

N
W E
S

Home Sweet Home

Anacondas are only found in South America. They live in warm and wet areas. Many of these big snakes live along the Amazon River in Brazil.

Anacondas always live near water. The anaconda is a very good, fast swimmer. Sometimes this snake is called a water boa. It's easy to see why!

Fun Fact!
Anacondas can stay completely underwater for more than 10 minutes.

Producing Young

Male and female anacondas mate once each year. Many males may try to mate with one female. Mating can last up to four weeks. Six months later, the female gives birth to a **brood** of live babies.

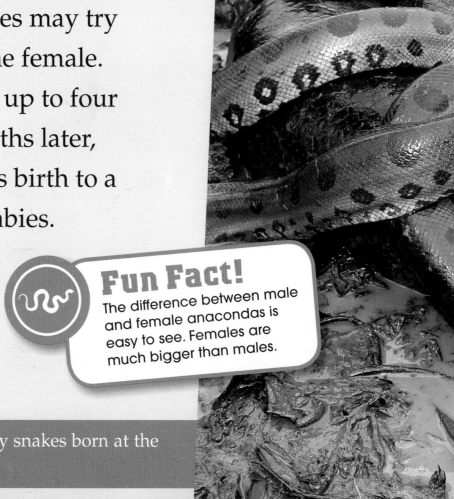

Fun Fact!
The difference between male and female anacondas is easy to see. Females are much bigger than males.

brood: a group of baby snakes born at the same time

Life Cycle of an Anaconda

Newborn
Baby anacondas are about 2 feet (0.6 meter) long.

Young
Young anacondas eat fish, frogs, and small rodents.

Adult
Male and female anacondas mate in the spring.

Growing Up

The size of the brood depends on the size of the mother anaconda. Females can give birth to between 14 to 82 baby snakes at one time. The young snakes hunt and take care of themselves right away. In three to four years, they will be fully grown and ready to mate.

Fun Fact!
Young anacondas face many dangers, even from their own mothers. Adults often eat baby snakes.

What's for Dinner?

Like all snakes, anacondas are meat eaters. Their favorite foods are fish, turtles, and birds. They can also eat very large prey like wild pigs and deer.

Fun Fact!
Anacondas swallow their prey whole.

Anacondas hunt at night. An
anaconda hides in the water and waits.
When an animal comes near, the snake
moves very quickly and grabs it.

Big Mouth

How can anacondas swallow big animals like pigs? The secret is in their special jaws. Snakes can stretch their jaws very wide.

In 1960, hunters in Brazil shot a huge anaconda. The snake was 27 feet, 9 inches (8.5 meters) long. It measured 44 inches (112 centimeters) around its body. The snake was never weighed. Scientists believe it weighed about 500 pounds (227 kilograms). That is one BIG snake!

21

Glossary

brood (BROOHD) — a group of young animals born at the same time

cold-blooded (KOHLD-BLUH-id) — having a body temperature that changes with the surroundings

constrict (kuhn-STRIKT) — to squeeze tightly to limit or prevent breathing

predator (PREH-duh-tor) — an animal that hunts other animals for food

prey (PRAY) — an animal hunted by another animal for food

reptile (REP-tile) — a cold-blooded animal that breathes air and has a backbone

Read More

Smith, Molly. *Green Anaconda: The World's Heaviest Snake.* SuperSized! New York: Bearport, 2007.

Thomson, Sarah L. *Amazing Snakes!* An I Can Read Book. New York: HarperCollins, 2006.

Woodward, John. *Boas.* Nature's Children. Danbury, Conn.: Grolier, 2004.

Internet Sites

FactHound offers a safe, fun way to find Internet sites related to this book. All of the sites on FactHound have been researched by our staff.

Here's how:
1. Visit *www.facthound.com*
2. Choose your grade level.
3. Type in this book ID **1429619201** for age-appropriate sites. You may also browse subjects by clicking on letters, or by clicking on pictures and words.
4. Click on the **Fetch It** button.

FactHound will fetch the best sites for you!

Index